Midnight B
and Other Juxtapositions

Carole Johnston

abuddhapress@yahoo.com

ISBN: 9798387320408

Midnight Butterfly is an oxymoron, creatively juxtaposed with several different situations and scenes. Some of the poems are metaphors and some are social satire. Many are just whimsical. All of the poems are either tanka or sedoka, Japanese short form.

Introduction

Think of "Midnight Butterfly" as an homage to Richard Brautigan's, *Trout Fishing In America*, a challenge to the surrealistic imagination.

A few years ago, I posted these poems to a website called "Lexington Poetry Month," where poets from Lexington, Kentucky share one poem each day in the month of June. I decided to challenge myself to write at least 30 poems, using the words or allusions to the nonsense phrase, "Midnight Butterfly." Midnight juxtaposed with Butterfly becomes an oxymoron and each poem uses the phrase in a different context.

These five and six line poems are not about butterflies or "Madam Butterfly" or lovers at midnight. Some of them do not make sense and some of them make sense as metaphors. All of them were fun to write. I hope you will have as much fun reading them.

Poems numbered 2, 6,11,14,25, and 9 were published in *Alien Buddha* Zine #38.

riding the
Midnight Butterfly Express
wearing my
glassy glitter wings I
wonder why everyone
reaches out to touch me

drummer in the
Midnight Butterfly Blues Band
heart beats neon
while a blind poet
misses the light show

got a letter
from Midnight Butterfly
tattered and worn
hand painted haiku moon
stained by indigo blood

wrote a book
called "Midnight Butterfly"
in secret code
all my horrors hidden
between the lines

jetting in my
Midnight Butterfly car
radio maniac
blaring cosmic questions
I hear myself on the wind

lost again
at Midnight Butterfly
Coffee Shop
scribbling runes in my notebook
with skyblueliminous ink

"Circus of the Soul"
starring Midnight Butterfly
run away with me
to the light show of your mind
at the poetry bizarre

in line at Starbucks
Midnight Butterfly taps
me on the shoulder
a poem pops in my mind
steams off in a coffee cloud

some say
Midnight Butterfly is just
a metaphor
muse in an old photograph
your smokey absinth dreams

wish I could paint
chiaroscuro lightning like
Midnight Butterfly
Joan Jet and Black Hearts
silver studs leather jackets

Kerouac and I
hitch with Midnight Butterfly
hiking toward dawn
thumbs out open highway
Basho in his green car

that carousel
my childhood in hyper-drive
a gold ring quest
chasing Midnight Butterfly
on glossy white horse
into the distant blue sea

you're drowning
in electric depression
Midnight Butterfly
writes you into a poem
hero with peacock blue ink

Midnight Butterfly
cruising in her flame green car
picking up angels
and poets in the dark - their
thumbs out on the open road
I hitch along for the ride

moonlight boogie
with Midnight Butterfly
star hopping
down the road toward solstice
leave your "ugly" at the door

Midnight Butterfly
following her bliss
savior in the summer dark
of our collective minds
a seer beyond the myth

dreamed I was
a butterfly at midnight
enchanted
by the glittering dark
like ancient Chuang Tau
wondering what was real

in that famous
dream Change Tzu became
confused
did the butterfly also dream
he was Chuang Tzu

if I dream
I am a butterfly
at midnight
will I forget that once
I couldn't fly?

am I the butterfly
or just a midnight dreamer
identity lost
in glamorous flight?
close your eyes and wonder

on the road
with Midnight Butterfly Jack
wondering
if we're just a metaphor
rambling through your dreams

on the corner
Midnight Butterfly Jack
his sign says
"homeless and hungry" I give
him a handful of stars

shape-shifting
with Midnight Butterfly
right now I
can feel the wings itching
to pierce through my skin

moon green
she blooms wide wings
neon like a ghost moth
glittering midnight

wings filled
with pale green ichor
she flies
only at midnight
lives only for love

once at midnight
I saw some moths
careening…Kamikaze
at the light trailing tails of
fire like dragon breath obsessed

gunman speaks
ghost voice dredged up
from wells of hate
stark uranium eyes sting
dark wings flutter over us

midnight girl
sleeping on a park bench
stained glass wings
glitter in the dark like
a butterfly cathedral
no hate can break her

she rises
to tangerine-rose-melon
dawnbreak
paints her midnight dreams
with monarch wings and tears
stained by the death of myth

after the dirge
a thousand butterflies
thunder up
like Thor at midnight
super héros - iron wings

just kids
we stashed caterpillars
in jars
dumped them on sidewalks
crushed them with our red Kids
no grace for butterflies

wrote a book
called Midnight Butterfly
metaphors
crept across pages
secret caterpillars
munching on manic truth

my butterfly brain
synapses fire at midnight…
neon zen laughter

Carole Johnston, poet, novelist and retired Creative Writing Teacher, lives in Lexington, Kentucky. She has published 3 books of poetry: **Journey's: Getting Lost** - Finishing Line Press, **Manic Dawn** - Wildflower Poetry Press, **Purple Ink - A Childhood in Tanka** - Finishing Line Press. She has also published many Japanese short form poems in a large variety of journals.

Printed in Great Britain
by Amazon

22276767R00040